herbst

herbst

Architecture in context
John Walsh

MASSEY UNIVERSITY PRESS

Contents

Introduction

In Aotearoa New Zealand the biggest challenges to architecture are those laid down by the landscape. These are tests not just of talent but also of temperament. It's easy to recognise the opportunity presented by a design commission for a building in a naturally beautiful place; harder to assume the responsibilities that go with the building's realisation. Considering its context, the building had better be good.

Over the past two decades, in a series of coastal and rural houses, the Tāmaki Makaurau Auckland architecture practice led by Lance and Nicola Herbst has consistently produced buildings that rise to the occasion of their extraordinary situation. Their body of work is a record of sequential excellence in a genre of particular cultural resonance in New Zealand; its appeal, though, is universal.

The Herbsts' success is such that, locally, they've achieved synonymity. The contemporary holiday house in New Zealand's temperate northern regions; sited sympathetically, constructed legibly and detailed painstakingly; protected from the weather while responsive to the environment; designed for casual but not indolent occupation, with mode shifts requiring manual intervention; disciplined in form but not meagre in material selection, with timber lending levity and masonry a countervailing gravity: what is the name of this thing? It's a 'Herbst bach'.

The sobriquet signifies the very deliberate, self-consciously aware application of exacting design standards to a building type that traditionally had no architectural pretensions whatsoever. For much of its twentieth-century existence, the New Zealand holiday house—the 'bach'—was basic. At best, it was carpenter-constructed, but often it was owner-built, put together from materials that were scavenged or scrounged, and altered or augmented when there was some money to spare. The bach was a retreat, a relaxed wellness centre where Nature was the therapist. Sunrise, sunset, high tide, low tide—those were the beats in the rhythm of bach days. On holiday at the bach standards could slip; the crockery was cracked and the furniture mismatched, threadbare shorts were everyday wear, and shoes and socks were gross contraventions of an unwritten sumptuary code.

The bach, then, was a variant of an archetype, the dwelling identified by the British architectural historian Joseph Rykwert as 'Adam's house in paradise'. Many countries and cultures have their own vernacular expression of prelapsarian simplicity: the cabin in the woods, the shack by the sea, the chalet in the mountains. Settler societies are especially inclined to folklorise a version of 'Adam's house', unsurprisingly, as the structure was the shape of freedom in a New World. Literally and figuratively, a family had made it. They had laid claim to a little patch of paradise.

In New Zealand, for these and all sorts of other reasons—the combination of a lot of coast and a small population; the colonial individualisation of indigenous collective ownership that, for a period, put possession of coastal property within even petit-bourgeois reach; a suburban society's ambivalence about urbanity; an ingrained enthusiasm for do-it-yourself pursuits—the bach, in the post-war decades, was an object of widespread desire. It mightn't have been much to look at but, culturally, it was a pheromone.

Herbst Architects' engagement with the bach and, more importantly, with what the bach represents, has endured for more than 20 years now. Beginning as a bit of crush on a type, it evolved into a sustained attempt to manifest essence in architecture, a long-term Platonic relationship, you could say. Even as circumstances changed—their own architectural aspirations, clients' appetite for amenity, and councils' recourse to prescriptive regulation all growing, over the years—the Herbsts have remained invested in the idea of the bach. The paradoxes inherent in this commitment, the sense of a trope under tension, make the work of Herbst Architects only more compelling. Can simplicity survive when it is rendered with such sophistication? Can informality co-exist with so strong an instinct for order? Can a bach be big?

And then there's the question of beauty. As far as the bach was concerned, beauty was beside the point. It matters to Lance and Nicola Herbst, though, and this explicit concern is distinctive in a profession typically reticent on the subject. In an arena of performative pragmatists—tough-guy developers, sceptical builders, stickler bureaucrats—architects are wary of being marginalised as the advocates for aesthetics. (They weren't always so coy: in his treatise, seminal to the Western canon, the Augustan-era Roman architect and combat engineer Vitruvius had no compunction in identifying beauty as a defining architectural quality.) Do the Herbsts set out to make beautiful buildings? 'Yes, no doubt about that,' says Nicola Herbst. 'Is that so unusual?'

Converts to a creed tend to be more ardent than those born into belief. What the Herbsts brought to a building type accorded rote recognition was a fresh gaze. The couple moved to New Zealand from South Africa in the late 1990s, coincidentally a time, as Nicola Herbst says, when the traditional Kiwi bach, although still secure as a cultural icon, was becoming an endangered species. The suburbanisation of many beach settlements was well under way, and in these places new houses were no different from those in the city. As well, a new stratum of vacation architecture was emerging: large houses in remote places, designed and built to meet the expectations of a clientele that was just as likely to be to be international as local.

Changing countries is not easy, but in retrospect the Herbsts' migration is a serendipitous case of just-in-time career, and life, management. The bach was sufficiently extant to inspire their architectural interest, and they were fortunate, and determined, enough to find on Aotea Great Barrier Island the perfect place to conduct their own prolonged interrogation of the type. In professional and personal terms, they'd found what they'd been looking for.

Both of the Herbsts are from Cape Town. They went to architecture school there and spent some years working for local practices, in the tumultuous period when power was being wrested from the National Party, which for almost half a century had institutionalised apartheid in South Africa. Nicola Herbst's path into architecture was relatively straightforward, a journey encouraged by supportive parents, especially by her capable and politically liberal mother, and at high school influenced by a passionate teacher who recognised her artistic ability. Her early appreciation for architecture was more a product of osmosis than education. The family home, when Nicola was a teenager, was a well-designed late-modernist rendition of the familiar Cape combination of solid masonry base and walls, and timber window frames and exposed ceiling rafters. 'I think my interest in architecture would have started there,' she says. From high school, Nicola went straight into the School of Architecture at the University of Cape Town (UCT), where she met Lance, her future partner in life and work.

Lance's progress into the profession was less direct. At Cape Town's South African College High School (SACS), an institution conscious of its venerable status as the country's oldest secondary school, he was an able student who was also good at sports, the latter a prized attribute at SACS. But, he says, he was restless, and rarely felt challenged. He does recall, though, an exceptional geography teacher and a librarian 'who fed me more and more advanced books'.

Then, two years of conscription—the mandatory military service imposed on white male high school graduates. When Lance came out the other end of an experience he describes as 'all bad', he found new friends. Several were the children of architects; one of the parents offered to take him on for a year as a draughtsman to see if he liked the work. He found it 'invigorating', he says, and decided to apply for architecture school. Acceptance depended on an art portfolio. 'I didn't have one, but I had become interested in photography so submitted a portfolio entirely of photographs. Miraculously, I was accepted.'

In the 1980s the architecture school at UCT was Bauhaus-like in the intensity of its studio-based pedagogy—'high pressure, but in a good way,' Lance says. 'You entered the school, and some years later you popped out, without ever seeming to have gone to sleep.' The internet was not yet around to distract the attention of students or dilute the influence of their teachers. The school's senior staff members were leading figures in contemporary South African architecture, inspirational teachers such as Roelof Uytenbogaardt

(1933–1988), Ivor Prinsloo (1935–2002) and Norbert Rozendal (1943–1995), who combined academia and successful practice.

It was a time of 'isms' at UCT, as at architectural academies everywhere, rationalism having been well and truly superseded by post-modernism and then by deconstructivism. But Uytenbogaardt in particular, although he latterly softened the linearity of his concrete architecture with the gentle curve so locally characteristic it was dubbed the 'Cape Town wiggle', kept enough of the modernist faith to pass it on. Nicola Herbst liked the 'rigour and elegant legibility' of Uytenbogaardt's architecture and admired the work of another Cape Town architect, Gawie Fagan (1925–2020), whose masonry-and-timber buildings were hybrids of modernist clarity and liquid shape-making.

In his architecture, Fagan ventured into the formal territory mapped by Le Corbusier, at Ronchamp, for example. From the look of some barrel-vaulted buildings he designed in the 1970s and 1980s, he was also impressed by Louis Kahn's Kimbell Art Museum (Fort Worth, Texas, 1972). At the same time, Fagan's work overtly referenced the gabled buildings of the Cape Dutch tradition. Acclaimed for his contemporisation of vernacular precedents, Fagan also offered lessons in the economic achievement of graceful effect. A hallmark of his architecture, notes South African architectural historian Arthur Barker, was the use of the flitch beam, in which a steel plate is sandwiched between timber beams to fashion rafters that provide strong support without obtrusive heft.

The Herbsts were paying attention: the flitch beam was later to be an important enabler of their timber architecture. 'At university I was fascinated by the combination of steel and timber,' Lance says, and actualising that fascination turned out to be a career-long commitment. In a tectonic sense, the Herbsts' practice in New Zealand has been 'twenty years of experimentation in refining how timber should work with steel'. At architecture school, Lance was a close student, too, of the work of Alvar Aalto. Footnotes to that fascination are the trusses at the Herbsts' Under Pōhutukawa (see pages 71–85), which suggest the timber butterfly trusses at Aalto's Säynätsalo Town Hall (1952).

At the time the Herbsts were students, the best buildings in Cape Town, designed by the best architects, were civic buildings, not private houses. (They were surprised when they came to New Zealand that the house was such a focus of architectural attention.) 'It was the grander realm of architecture we were trained in and taught to be concerned about,' Nicola says. But it was architecture at the other end of the scale that was more enduringly affective. 'My family was lucky enough to have access to buildings that were kind of equivalent to the New Zealand bach,' she says. Nicola would visit one coastal property with several rondavels, the small, cylindrical, thatched-roof structures common in southern Africa. Closer to Cape Town, there was a fibre-cement shack, sitting on a concrete base, with an outside long-drop toilet, with spiders and snakes. 'You could open a door and listen to the sea,' Nicola remembers. 'I went there throughout my childhood and into my twenties. It's very evocative for me—a touchstone.'

After graduation, Nicola worked for a large Cape Town architecture firm that specialised in high-rise buildings—'bold, and rather ostentatious', she says 'with quite a bit of marble in every foyer'. Lance was offered a job by the architect who had first employed him, and for whom he had made models in university breaks. The position was in fact a partnership; on reflection, Lance says, it was a bit much at that stage of his career. After two years, he says, he decided 'to do my own thing, working at home at the dining table, designing alterations and additions'. For a while, he worked with Nicola's brother, Andrew Meiring, who is also an architect. Together they set up a small multi-disciplinary practice, finding commissions through their social network.

Lance was restless, though, and ready for a new start somewhere else; the experience of conscription had left him disenchanted with South Africa. The prospect of departure was more daunting for Nicola, whose ties to her homeland and close family were stronger. New Zealand was possible, in the mid-1990s, as a migration destination, and the Herbsts successfully applied for admission. (Some years later, Nicola's family, including her twin sister, Jackie Meiring, a photographer who took many of the photographs in this book, joined her in New Zealand.) For a few years, the couple's life was an unsettled round of coming and going as they attended to work in New Zealand and unfinished personal business in South Africa. At one stage, Lance was sitting in an office in Cape Town designing a waterfront hotel in Auckland.

What made the Herbsts' move definitive was their discovery and purchase of a small section of land on Aotea Great Barrier, the largest of the islands in Tīkapa Moana Hauraki Gulf, and the most remote from Auckland city. (It takes more than four hours on a ferry, or 30 minutes on a very small plane, to travel the 100-kilometre distance.) They visited the sparsely populated island when one of their Auckland commercial clients asked them to design a bach there. The Herbsts bought a bit of land on the same beach, just before the value of Aotea coastal real estate commenced its inexorable rise.

'We really had to put some roots down,' Nicola says. 'We needed a place that would give us an emotional connection to this country, and that would be a source of happiness.' For nearly a quarter of a century, the bach the Herbsts designed and built for themselves on Aotea (pages 23–37) has been their retreat, and the test site for their architectural ideas. They've been the subjects of their own experiment. In a profound way, the Herbsts' Aotea bach made their life in a new country possible, Nicola says. They never thought it would also be integral to the evolution of their architectural practice.

In the 25 years since they opened their architectural account on Aotea, the Herbsts have gone on to design more than a dozen holiday houses there. Such is the strength of their Aotea reputation that other architecture firms must know that to practise on the island is to invite invidious comparison. In addition to these Aotea baches, and other holiday houses in other places, Herbst Architects designed different types of buildings—offices, warehouses, apartments and even, perhaps as homage to that kindly librarian of Lance's schooldays, a small primary school library. The practice took on these commercial projects, sites of design compromise, not experiment, until the increasing value of their residential commissions meant they could leave them behind.

For more than a decade, commercial work effectively subsidised the Herbsts' bach work, buying the architects time to apply their innate perfectionism to a building type rarely flattered by such attention, and to educate themselves in the performance and possibilities of a medium new to them. 'In South Africa we had hardly worked with wood,' Lance says. 'Roofs had timber but there was no such thing as a timber wall or timber cladding. It was just brick and concrete.'

The Herbsts came to New Zealand as well-taught architects, but migration made them autodidacts. Of course they were familiar with architecture's universal principles, but they didn't know about the local particulars. They weren't steeped in the precedents of what architect and critic David Mitchell called New Zealand architecture's 'carpenter tradition'. The upside? 'We had no baggage,' Nicola says. 'We weren't constrained by preconceptions of how things should and shouldn't be done.'

In their early baches, the Herbsts proceeded to piece things together, determined to let the timber do the talking. This commitment to material fidelity—integral but not exclusive to modernism—was allied to a compulsive interest in the details of building assembly. The resulting architecture was as much an exercise in control as a controlled experiment. 'We were trying to develop a timber construction language,' Lance says, 'one that expressed honesty, rigour and order.' A meta language, in other words: the Herbsts were designing buildings about buildings.

The Herbsts' architectural temperament distanced them from the late-twentieth-century course taken by many architects in the city to which they had moved. In Auckland, examples of post-modern idiosyncrasy were easy to find, although a stricter regime was beginning to be introduced. Patrick Clifford's own Auckland home, the Clifford-Forsyth House (1995), for example, was an elegant realisation, in timber and concrete block, of coherent intent—a palate cleanser after an architectural binge session. The wider Antipodean context—and the Herbsts, since coming to New Zealand, have observed the confident progress of Australian architecture—evidenced the presence of kindred spirits. For example, what the Herbsts were doing with their bach on Aotea was similar to what Sydney architect

Peter Stutchbury was doing with houses at Pittwater and Shoalhaven on the New South Wales coast: crafting, with as sensitive a touch as possible, structures that combined sufficiency and seclusion, protection and permeability.

At first glance, the Herbsts' very disciplined approach to bach design seems to be a counter-intuitive response to a very casual type. But the architects have always understood that if a building is resolved, in its proportions, its inter-spatial connections and its details, it will be restful. And with their baches, from the earliest iterations onwards, the Herbsts have been careful not to construe clarity as austerity. Across a wide range of budgets, the baches have a richness, thanks to the exposition of their timber composition, and a depth, derived from the layered arrangement of decks, screens and shutters. The point, too, about Herbst baches, is that for all their composure, they exist in a relationship that demands deference. Nature makes the rules in the places where the Herbsts design their baches.

'We came from a very easy climate to a more difficult one,' Nicola says, 'but we still really wanted to spend our time outdoors.' So did their bach clients, although perhaps not quite to the extent the architects preferred. (In the Herbsts' early baches, minor inconveniences, such as a dash in the rain to an outside loo, were programmed in as features distinguishing holiday homes from city residences.) 'We learned very quicky that in New Zealand, you don't hide from the sun, you chase it,' Lance says. 'Then there's the frequent rain and constant wind.' To reconcile climate reality, as it applies in even the warmer regions of Auckland and North-land, with their design ideals and their clients' tolerance, Nicola says, 'the buildings just had to work harder'. That doesn't mean these buildings' inhabitants were off the hook. Herbst baches have quite a lot of moveable parts; owners must be prepared to be operators.

In designing their early baches, and their successor holiday houses, the Herbsts sought to establish the 'porous connection to nature' that they believe is fundamental to the bach experience. Their strategy involves a number of tactics: the veiling with slatted timber to provide a rain screen; the incising of many apertures, all requiring some cover; the deployment of alternative deck areas to accommodate wind shifts; the adaptation of the lanai, the Hawaiian roofed patio or veranda, as a sheltered exterior space. The latter element, especially, became endemic to the Herbsts' architecture; the adaptable room's many advantages include its programmatic utility. At the Awana Beach House, for example (pages 191–211), the lanai is the means of handling the transition between front and rear levels on a sloped site.

'We don't want a blatant separation of inside and out, a sense of severing,' Nicola says. At the same time, she says, 'we like to give substance to a threshold'. The inspiration the architects acknowledge here is the engawa, in traditional Japanese architecture the covered corridor running along a building's exterior. Like the lanai, the engawa is an in-between zone, providing shelter but accessible to the elements.

It's tempting to view the Herbsts, like the great Australian architect Glenn Murcutt, as architects of the touch-the-earth-lightly persuasion, and that perception is understandable if based only on a superstructural gaze at their earlier buildings. However, they've always been believers in embedding buildings in the ground. 'It's natural to us,' Lance says. Of course: the Herbsts grew up in a solid city built of earth stuff—brick and stone—and were taught by architects who designed masonry buildings. But for Lance, in particular, there's more to the matter than an inherited disposition. His hostility to the notion of architectural rootlessness is almost visceral. 'It's anathema to me that a building might look like it could walk off a site,' he says. (It's safe to say he won't be providing any testimonials for house relocation companies.)

In the early years of Herbst Architects, when budgets were smaller, the practice's timber baches were given the anchoring weight and unifying thread of gabion walls, long runs of river rocks encaged in wire baskets. As well as performing demarcation duty, gabion walls provide a textural service—stones, to go with all those sticks—and they have continued to characterise the Herbsts' architecture even as bigger budgets have allowed for earthworks, concrete walls and stone plinths. (See, for example, Dune House, pages 175–189, and Omata Beach House, pages 213–235.) 'We've always wanted to dig buildings into the land, and now we're able to,' Lance says. Visits to Greece validated this already strong inclination. Not surprisingly; just as European philosophy has been described as a series of footnotes to Plato, so the Western architectural tradition can be seen to rest on the quarried stone of ancient Greece. It was, though, just as much the work of contemporary architects in Greece that impressed him, Lance says: 'The way they dig into a site is so interesting. The cuts are so positive—they set the language for the building.'

As their practice has developed, the Herbsts have increasingly demonstrated their readiness to dig into and re-form the ground under and around their buildings. They've had to: the buildings have been getting bigger, passing definitively in status from bach to house. Something else has also happened. The Herbsts' architecture, Lance says, has become more 'singular'. Again, this is, in part, a design response to the growth issue. An increase in scale easily leads, in architecture, to a loss of control—not a surrender the Herbsts would contemplate. 'For quite a while, we've been trying to strip things back, become simpler in form and more refined, less reliant on movement,' Lance says.

The progress toward singularity is recently evident in the Omata Beach House, completed in 2022, the largest of the Herbsts' holiday houses, and can be explicitly measured in the contrast between two houses, near-neighbours at Piha beach on Auckland's west coast: the wonderfully expressive Under Pōhutukawa, from 2010, and the coolly self-possessed Kawakawa House, completed in 2018 (pages 141–155). Castle Rock House, finished in 2015 (pages 87–105), sits halfway between the two, chronologically, but, with the elements of its form finely poised between fusion and fission, it is typologically closer to Under Pōhutukawa. A year later, with the completion of the Kauaeranga Valley House (pages 125–139), the needle of the dial of design intent had moved much further in the direction of singularity.

'Singularity' is the formal expression of a concept. In a way, the path of Herbst Architects' evolution has been an ascent from detail to concept. That's not to say that in the practice's contemporary work details are in any sense neglected; their importance remains a given and, if anything, the stakes involved in their resolution are even higher. The design tolerances of building components such as, for example, the glazed shutters, framed and tracked in aircraft-grade aluminium, that slide along the sea-facing front of the Awana Beach House (pages 191–211), are extremely exacting. It's just that details don't carry the same expository burden as they had in the Herbsts' earlier baches, which were smaller and cheaper.

Apart from a sensitivity to context that, from the start, has been a defining characteristic of the Herbsts' architecture, those buildings expressed the dynamics of a relatively straightforward relationship, that between an overarching idea—the 'bach'—and its material manifestation. God, to use Mies van der Rohe's phrase, was in the details.

As was the devil, especially as the baches got bigger. The Herbsts' own standards remained uncompromising as their buildings became more complicated. Client expectations rose in step with larger budgets. In the wake of New Zealand's turn-of-the-century leaky building crisis, councils decided that lowest common should be the denominator governing design discretion. (A curb on experiment was the unavoidable corollary of safeguards against incompetence; a thicker building envelope is more forgiving of imprecise detailing.) These factors were all prompts for the Herbsts to review their architecture, looking not so much at its dialectics as its dialect.

'In our buildings, we had been exploring a very "sticky" language, and its usage is demanding,' Lance says. He recalls a conversation with the Indian architect Bijoy Jain, founder of the acclaimed practice Studio Mumbai and a fellow obsessive about the minutiae of making. 'He was saying, "The tyranny of detail—it will kill you." The whole business of working things out—the junctions, the joinings, the fixings, the modelling of all of a building's meetings—can lead you into a wormhole. You've got to watch out.'

The way to pull back from the brink, for the Herbsts, has been to raise their gaze. They have become focused on the discovery of concepts that can drive the design of particular projects. Under Pōhutukawa, a house made to belong in the grove of native trees in which it sits, is, Lance says, 'probably the first time I said, "I'm really going to pursue a metaphor in the design of a building and see how it goes".' The intention was poetic, as was the design motive for Clevedon Estate (pages 107–123), a building addition realised as a 'gossamer' counterpoint to an existing heavyweight house.

The interpolation of a conceptual or metaphorical layer between the big idea—the 'bach'—and the details of specification and assembly has been important to the Herbsts' architecture. It has a generative formal potential that's entirely compatible with the Herbsts' pursuit of singularity, and it also takes the pressure off the 'bach' to provide the ideological context for the practice's work. Clearly, as the Herbsts' projects increased in scale and functional scope, too much was being asked of the 'bach' as descriptor or definer. Driven instead by a concept particular to its circumstances, a building can more truly be itself, not an iteration of a type.

The progress of the Herbsts' practice, always a close and mutually supportive partnership, has of course occurred as they have moved on through life. Even at their own house on Aotea, they have become less strict in their observance of their younger-self injunctions against too-comfortable bach life. 'We've been recalibrating the dial on convenience,' Nicola says. 'For example, we now enjoy having a covered walkway between some amenities.'

But aspects of the Herbsts' architectural belief have not lapsed: a house in a beautiful place should properly acknowledge its site; refuge should involve some renunciation of the regimes of normal life; habitation should bring joy. Each holiday house the Herbsts design is a candle lit on the altar of architecture to the spirit of the bach.

23 Herbst Bach Aotea Great Barrier 1999–

The summer after we had immigrated to New Zealand we spent a couple of weeks in a caravan on Aotea Great Barrier. The island, out on the edge of the Hauraki Gulf, 100 kilometres from Auckland, immediately resonated with us. It was undeveloped and its buildings were not at all pretentious. Land on Aotea was more affordable then and we were able to buy the site next to where we had stayed. Designing and building our bach was a way to root ourselves in this country.

We felt at ease with the bach type, and probably even romanticised it. We were familiar with similar buildings in South Africa, made from different materials and for a different climate but just as straightforward and unfussy—informal and accretive, definitely not like city houses or the big holiday houses on the beaches near Cape Town.

The bach on Aotea wasn't meant to be a 'proper' building. We were interested in smallness and sufficiency, and wanted an informal connection with nature. At first, the bach was basic, almost a diagram for the provision of the necessities—shelter, water, cooking—that allowed us to get on with the rituals of a holiday. Things developed from there (although we've only just got a washing machine).

The Aotea bach is a grouping of parts or, you could say, an arrangement of inconveniences. To us, physical engagement with both building and site is integral to bach life, a point of difference to the sedentary occupation of an urban or suburban home, and we try to programme it into our beach architecture. Even as our baches have grown into beach houses, we've tried to hold onto this analogue, hands-on quality. What do people remember from childhood days at the bach? Simple things, like helping Dad clean the fish he'd caught or doing the dishes with your brothers and sisters or, perhaps, the journey in the dark to the long-drop toilet at the back of the garden. Life at the beach is about experiences, not stuff. LH • NH

MAORI
BILL BRYSON
IRVINE WELSH GLUE
ELIF SHAFAK
IAN McEWAN SOLAR
MAGNUMMAGNUM
READING MAGNUM
A YEAR
IN PHOTOGRAPHY
MAGNUM ARCHIVE
fish
AROH
S

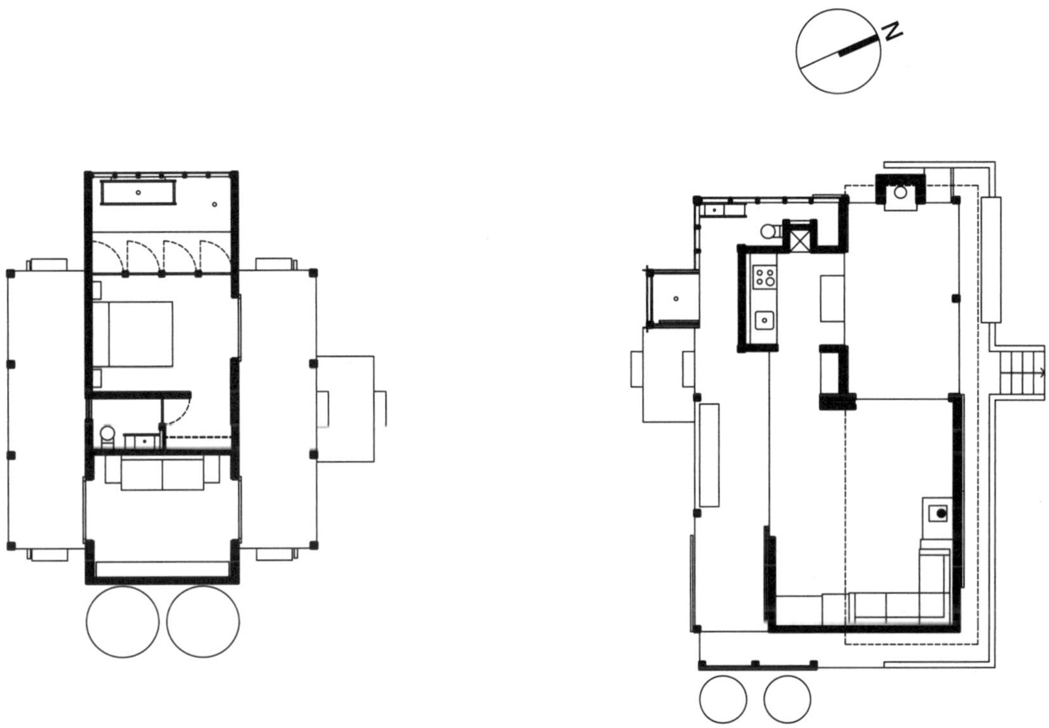
N

39

Ōruawharo Bay Bach
Aotea Great Barrier
2008

When we came to design this house, we thought we had some answers to the questions of bach living; after all, we had tested ideas on our own place. This was the first time, though, that we explored for a client the notion of a building made of small pieces, of providing less, not more. The client understands Aotea: it's not easy to get to the island, and building there is even harder. If you're up for that challenge, you're already in our camp.

The building has two parts, a horizontal pavilion and a tower, with an outside area in between. This was our original use of what was to become a consistent element of our beach architecture: the lanai, a roofed space accommodating a dining table and fire. The lanai is the heart of the bach; the structures surrounding it are there essentially to define its edges.

We had come from a continental country with stable weather but in New Zealand we quickly understood that coastal buildings require layers of defence. At Ōruawharo Bay, much of our thinking was around how the bach could reverse itself to handle both El Niño winds from the south and west and La Niña winds from the northeast. Accordingly, the building has two decks and the kitchen relates to both equally well.

The relationship of the kitchen to the lanai is enabled by the solid spine of a gabion wall—stones encaged in steel mesh—that binds the bach's loose collection of forms together. This gabion wall was a lesson in what weight does as a holding element and, like the lanai, it has been a recuring element in our beach houses.

In South Africa, you can do without a waterproof covering over an outside space, but not in New Zealand. So, how to make a covering not feel like a roof? Glass-fibre sheets, with battens underneath, admit light, and under this protection you still feel you're outside. It's important that the outdoor spaces of a bach don't take on the character of badly appointed inside spaces. A deck should be distinct from the interior floor—its timber should be rougher, its planks not so perfectly planed. If a breeze comes up through the deck, then roll out a carpet (as we do at our own bach). LH • NH

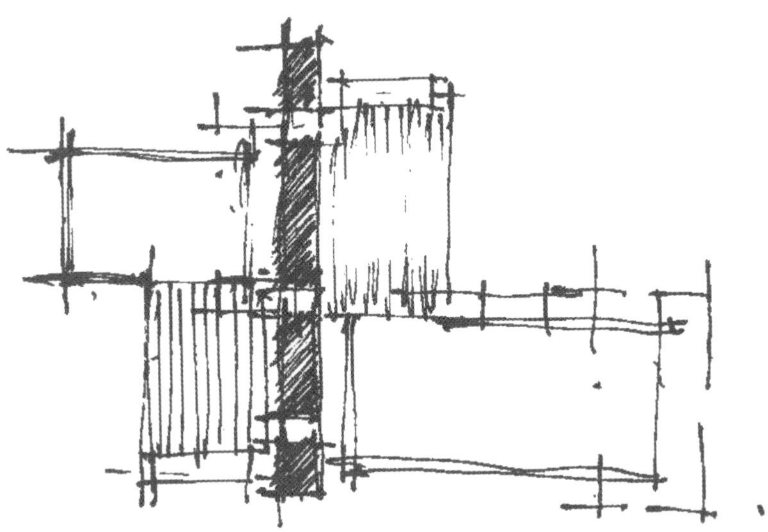

BEACH

Upper Floor
Lower Floor

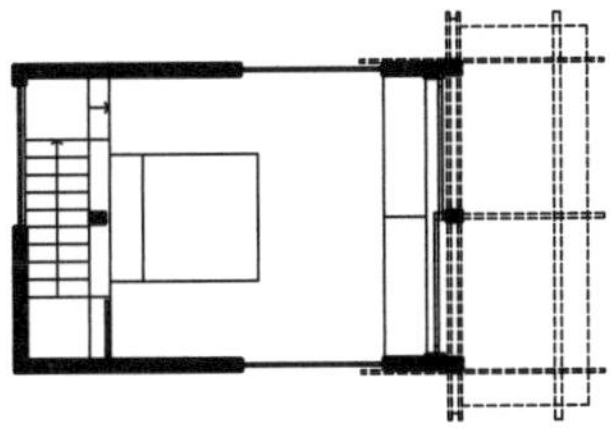

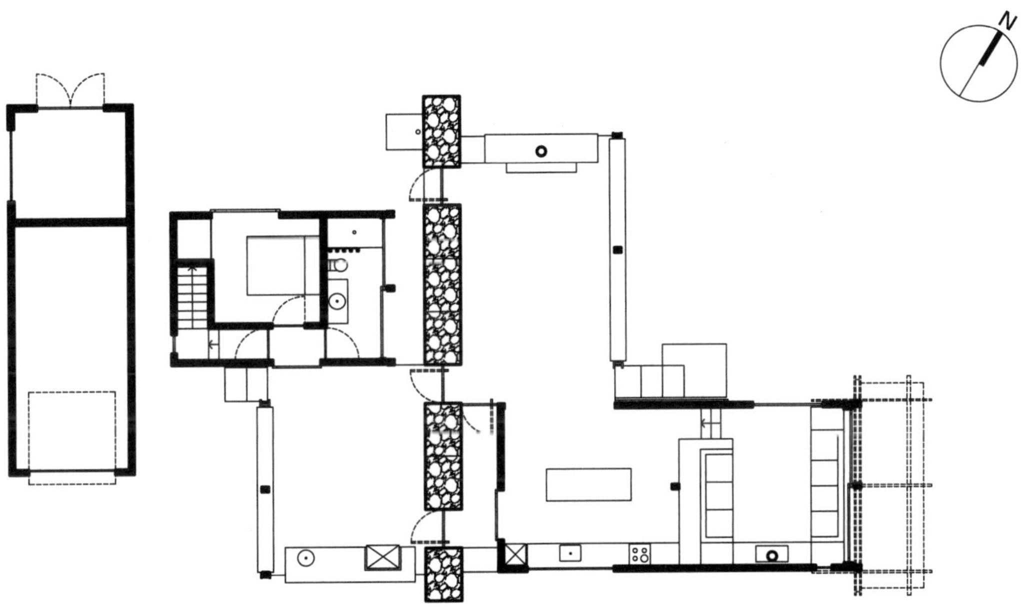

Kaitoke Bach
Aotea Great Barrier
2011

The bach is in a row of houses, close to its neighbours. A linear block containing the bedrooms runs along one boundary; on the other, protection is provided by a gabion wall. A right-angled roof connects the two forms and frames the lanai, itself a gateway to a private foreground—a lens through which to view Hirakimatā Mount Hobson, the highest peak on Aotea. All of the bedrooms are accessed from the outside passage; if access was internal, the bach would have become less 'bachy'. Shutters give shelter and control light.

When we came to New Zealand and saw houses being uplifted and trucked away to new sites, we couldn't believe it. Aren't buildings markers of a particular time and place? Surely you can't uproot a house? Even though we were designing very light buildings, such as Kaitoke Bach, we wanted to embed them in the land. That's why we have often used gabion walling. It's a road retaining system, usually, but with bach architecture you're often wanting, or needing, to be creative with materials originally intended for another purpose. Gabions have the utility and effect of a rock wall, but for less expense.

We first used gabions to hide the undersides of a deck and then started to incorporate them as structural walls that, with their weight and mass and in the depth of their openings, gave substance and shadow to lightweight timber buildings. The gabions became textural, space-making elements that connected a building to the land.

Architecture is about gravity. It is also about proportion. Buildings must have the strength to stay up, but the eye doesn't make allowances for measures taken to meet the seismic code. Disproportionate mass registers as clumsiness. In timber structures such as the Kaitoke Bach, steel flitches in the centre of posts and beams allow building elements to be strong enough to perform seismically while retaining the slender proportions that the eye perceives as appropriate to a bach's hierarchy of heft. LH•NH

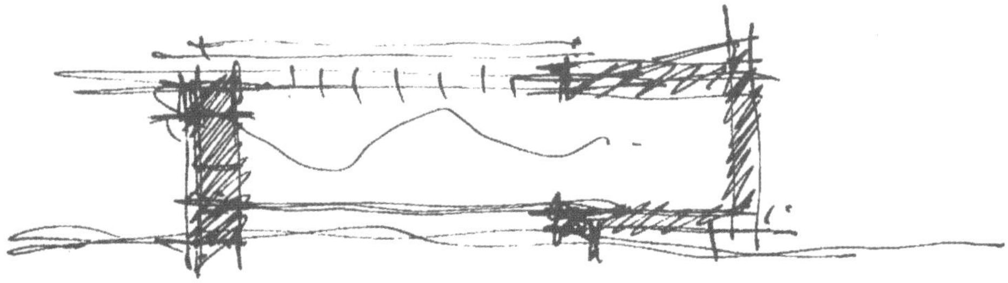

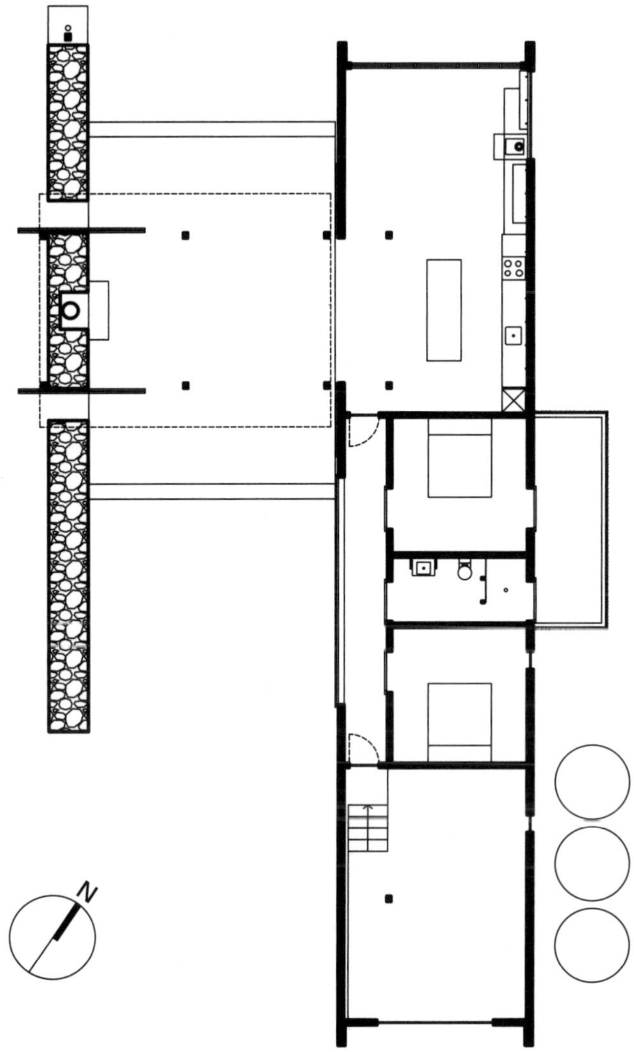
N

71 Under Pōhutukawa
Piha
2011

Our clients for this beach house, who are architecture enthusiasts, were very supportive even though, they later told us, they had thought they might not be able to get consent for a house on a site covered in mature pōhutukawa trees. Piha is a close-knit and environmentally conscious community. We realised the only way we were going to gain council consent and community acceptance was to make poetry.

To make space for the house we did have to cut down some trees, as few as was necessary. We wanted to establish a strong relationship between the house and the surviving trees. In a sense, these trees were the client; we felt that we were in their debt, and believed we had to try to make the house as beautiful as the pōhutukawa.

The building, simply, is two towers connected by a lightweight roof. The cladding is dark-stained cedar, deployed as battens—a rendition of the bark of pōhutukawa. We usually shy away from decoration, but here, as we were searching for the poetic, we embraced metaphor: the cladding of the towers alludes to the dark-barked trunk of pōhutukawa and the house's interior plywood lining to the lighter-coloured heartwood of cut trees.

The roof that connects the towers, and which is cantilevered at double-storey height to shelter the living spaces that flow out to the decks, is the house's canopy. The struts supporting the glazed roof are the house's branches. The proportions of these 'branches' had to be right; the struts are seismically essential, but if they were too thick the canopy effect would have failed.

This is a glassy building; its shutters are the trees that surround it. We try to avoid walls of glass—they are too demanding to live with—but the surrounding pōhutukawa made this much glazing possible. At this house, what is building and what isn't building, what is inside and what is outside, becomes ambiguous. You're not quite sure whether you're sitting under the trees or sitting in the building. LH • NH

Upper Floor
Lower Floor

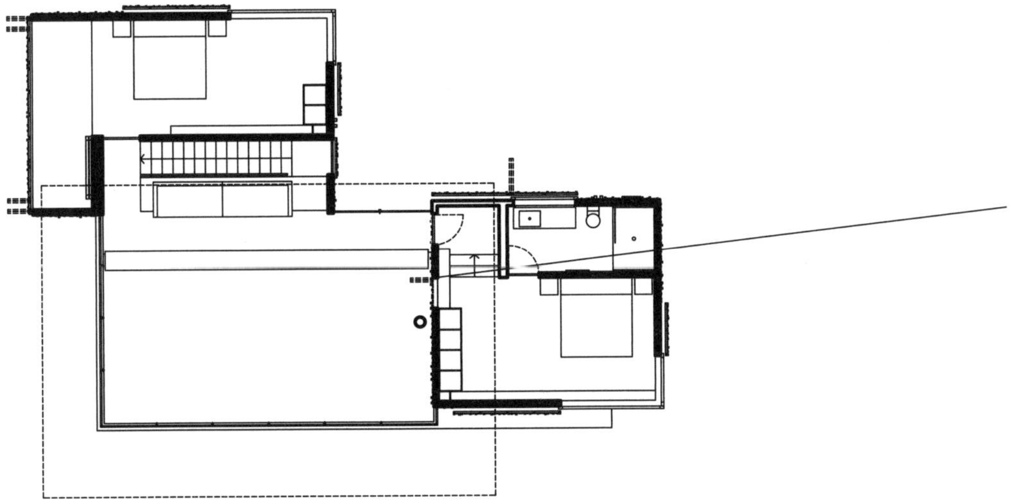

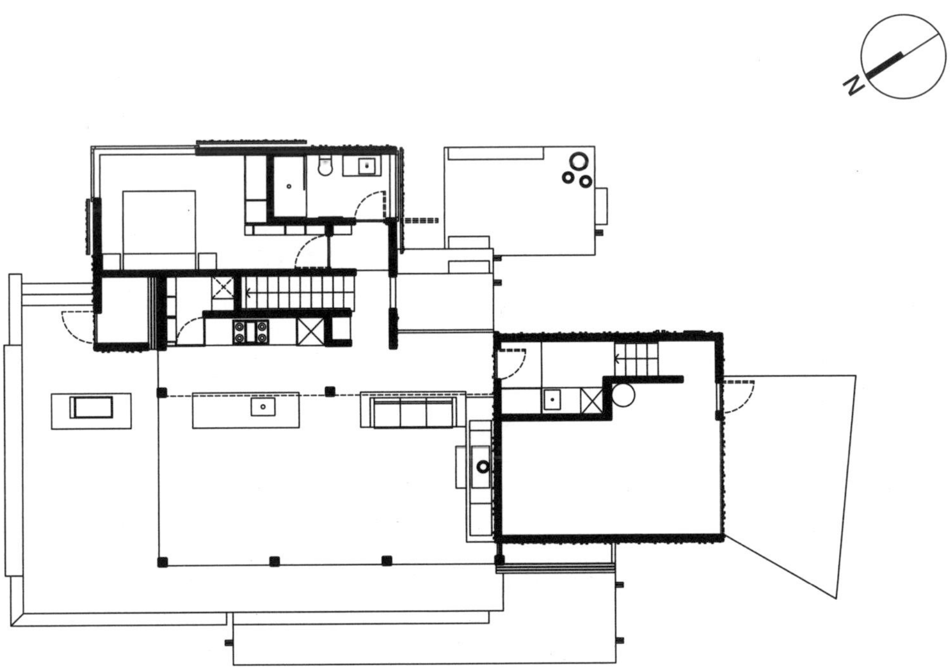

Castle Rock House
Whangārei Heads
2002

As our practice developed, our projects started to grow in scale and sophistication, graduating from bach to beach house. The Castle Rock House has three bedrooms and is clad in cedar, more expensive than pine, but a better performer in a maritime environment. But amidst the changes some things have remained the same. We always try to make houses smaller, and if we can't make them smaller, we break them up into smaller parts, as with this house. The Castle Rock House is embedded into the land by a gabion wall, which is also used as an organising principle for the design. External circulation to the bedrooms makes movement through the building a constant negotiation between inside and out.

The house is located on a hilly site with views south to the ocean and northeast to dominant Castle Rock, and has to operate in both directions. In plan, the living component of the house is four squares centred around a pinch-point connection to the bedroom wing. There are two decks and two lanais, one for each wind condition, and the kitchen also looks two ways; the sunken lounge is the place of refuge when outside is out of the question.

This was the first time we really started to work with rain screens, which we've now been doing for almost 20 years. One prompt was major changes to New Zealand's building legislation; in response to a 'leaky building crisis' the building code prescribed standard details, which tend to be clunky and unattractive. A rain screen deals with this, by hiding flashings, providing crisp edges, and giving depth to the façade. Used in conjunction with a lanai, it's a means of turning simple waterproof boxes into expressive timber buildings.

Recessive colours are encouraged, or even mandated, for highly visible houses on the New Zealand coast. That's fine with us: we like dark-stained timber, which goes with the dark bark of the native flora. It might not work in other parts of the world, but in Aotearoa many councils and landscapers want it, and clients are comfortable with it. LH•NH

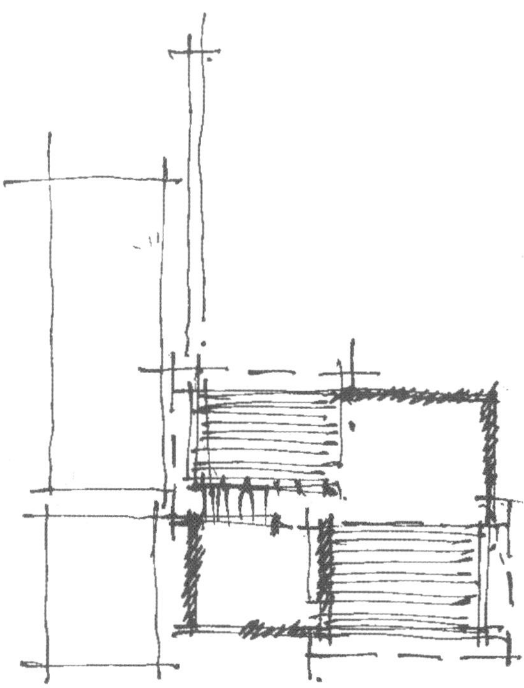

Othello

Upper Floor
Lower Floor

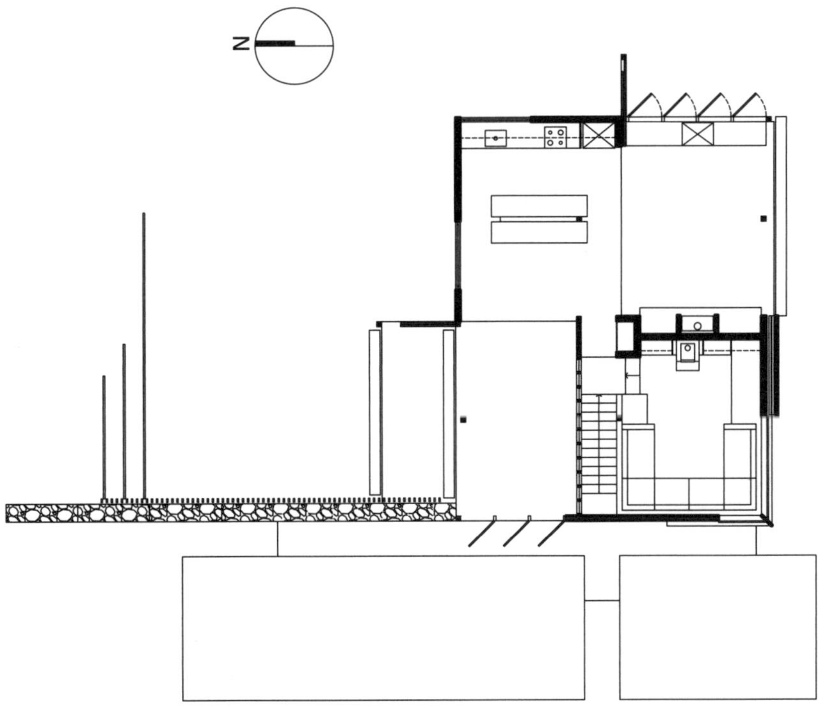

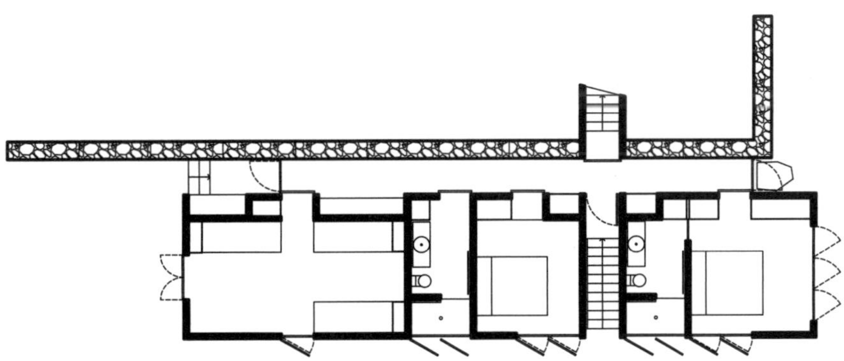

A generous budget, an encouraging client and a brief that really was brief allowed us to achieve something purely architectural—a structure that is almost architecture for the sake of architecture. The clients asked for some additions to their existing large stone building: a study and some storage space, and a place to park cars. The concise brief was liberating. Our baches have to work so hard; they might look simple but they are quite complicated and, at times, it felt as though we were obsessing on their performance. On this project we were freer to focus on architectural forms, to be more reductive.

When we first visited the house we realised that what it needed more than anything was a sense of arrival—the house is in the country and getting there is a journey. In a sense we invented a brief, designing a structure long enough to provide another edge to the entrance. This stops the space from seeming to slip away and instead frames an arrival courtyard.

The new building along this edge doesn't have solid walls but is almost entirely shuttered. It's the antithesis of the heavy stone house, its ghost. If the addition had been solid, there wouldn't be such a dynamic relationship between the buildings. Two notional bridges between the existing and the new building offer some cover; the formal role of these connections is to complete the square of the courtyard and provide a gateway to the entrance.

The addition has a concrete roof. There's an architectural thrill in such a gossamer building holding up this solid slab. Underneath the building, gabion walls provide anchoring weight. We designed large doors for the addition, smooth on what was to be their exterior face, and braced on the other side. When they arrived on site, the client suggested turning them around, a serendipitous intervention, as it turned out. LH • NH

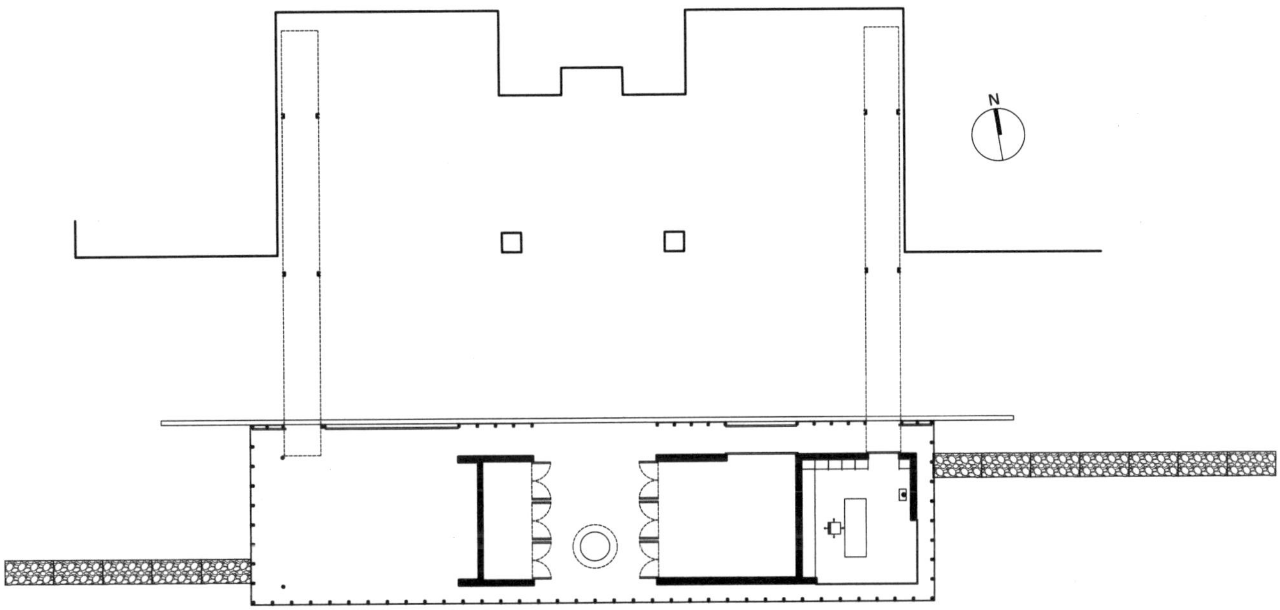
N

Kauaeranga Valley House
Coromandel
2016

One of architecture's truisms is that 'it's all about the clients'. It's rarely that simple, but on this project it really was all about the clients, a film-industry couple who spend a lot of time on location and wanted a house that would be a refuge. The clients came with a brief for a small house, which, of course, we welcomed. However, because the house is sited in a big rural valley, it seemed to us that it required a certain scale to hold its own against the challenge of the landscape.

The site selected for the house is on a slope above the valley. Projecting from this incline, the house shelters under a roof that is effectively the entire upper level of the two-storey building. This big hat encloses bedrooms and services at the end of the house anchored against the slope, and accommodates a double-height volume above the glazed platform of the living area at the other.

The clients, unsurprisingly, had a cinematic approach to the house's appearance. They wanted a building that looked aged and weathered, a bit beaten up. They had considered having their set designers distress the building, but it seemed to make sense to just start with beaten-up materials. Our scheme specified a rain screen over recycled timber, the job of the screen being, basically, to cover up the box behind it. As for the screen's composition—every farm in the house's vicinity has a rusted corrugated iron shed in a paddock. Why not use old iron for the rain screen?

It wasn't easy to find the right stuff—old iron is often too thin to salvage. The clients drove around the district looking for perfectly rusted two-millimetre-thick corrugated iron, eventually finding it on the roof of an old brewery. The building's owner was happy to trade his rusted iron for a new roof, if a bit bemused by the deal.

On our first visit to see the rain screen in place, we stopped by the road to take a photo. A ute pulled up, and the driver leaned out to say, 'Have you ever seen anything bloody worse than that in your whole life?' The young woman with him didn't agree. 'Nah,' she said. 'I love it.' LH • NH

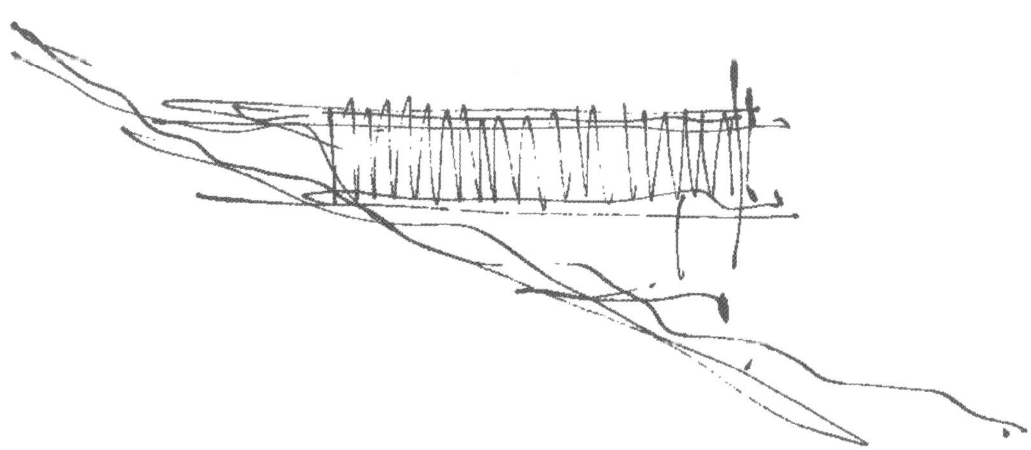

Upper Floor
Lower Floor

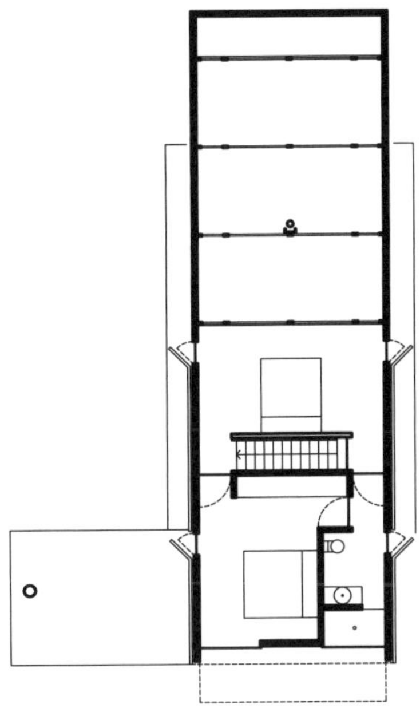

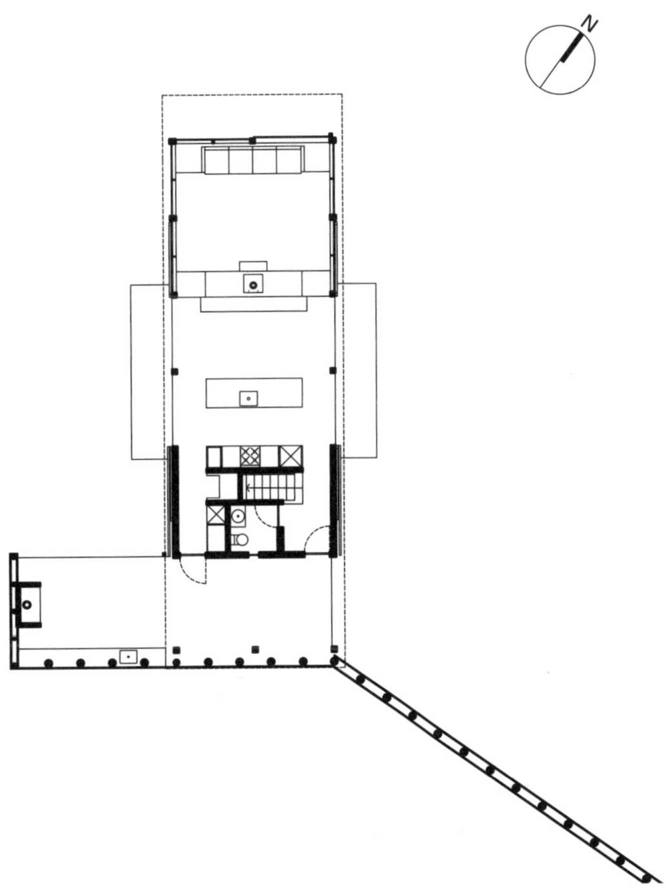

141

Kawakawa House
Piha
2018

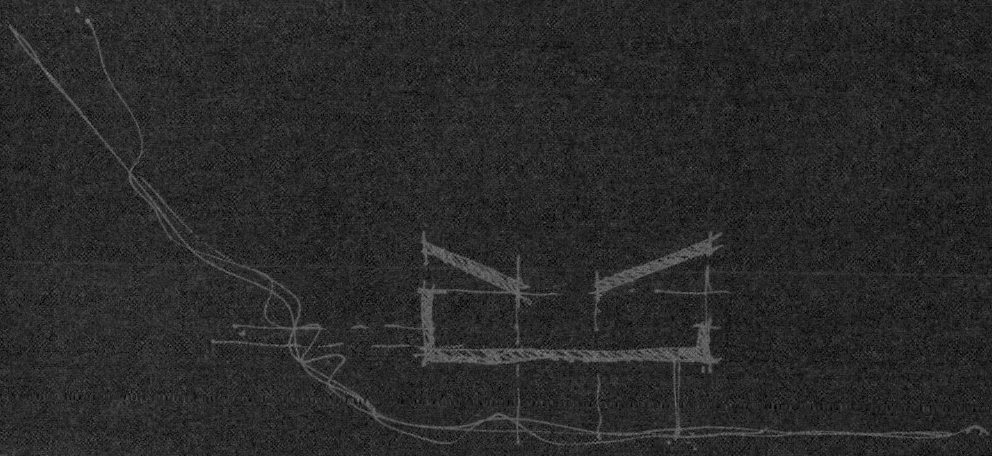

Kawakawa House sits among trees, but it's more birdcage than treehouse, or a reverse birdcage—one with people inside and the birds flying free.

The house is sited near the earlier Under Pōhutukawa, but because we were building on the footprint of an existing building there wasn't the same need to navigate around or remove mature trees. However, light was a challenge. The house is hard up against the steep hill that comes down to the beach, and even in summer loses the sun for much of the day.

To get a view of the beach and ocean the house had to rise above the dwelling in front. The whole building, really, is on the upper floor; there are only services on the ground level. We designed the front of the upper floor as a deck or platform that can be closed down—Auckland's west coast weather is often too bracing for elevated open-deck living. The deck reference is made more explicit by the balustrade that runs across the upper floor, inside the glazing line. The central courtyard is the focus for sheltered outside living.

The other imperative was letting in light from above while engaging with the tree canopy all the way around. The ceiling becomes like the top of a tree, its four planes sloping down towards the centre —a canopy separated by clerestory windows from the rest of the building below. The roof geometry was very demanding. Four pitches had to meet perfectly; in addition, the planes of the outer skin (roof) and inner skin (ceiling) meet at slightly different angles. 'Who built this roof?' a friend of the clients asked. 'A watchmaker?'

Concrete blockwork holds the entrance, services and spiral stair; this Corbusian trunk seemingly supports the cantilever over the carport. With its sharpness and clarity, the house has an affinity to a modernist pavilion, perhaps from mid-century California. Kawakawa House is probably our most single-minded, if not singular, building. LH•NH

EAT UP

Upper Floor
Lower Floor

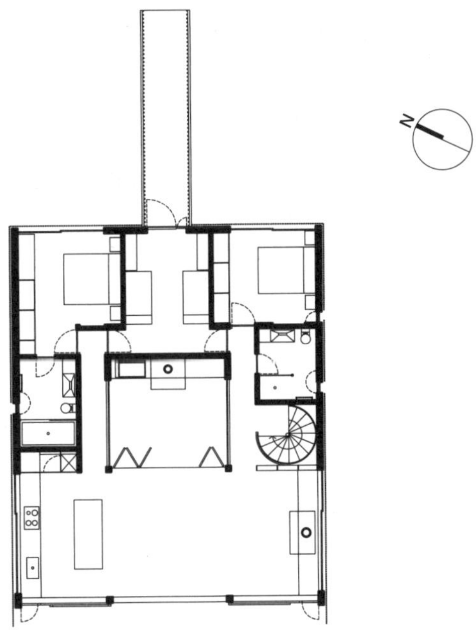

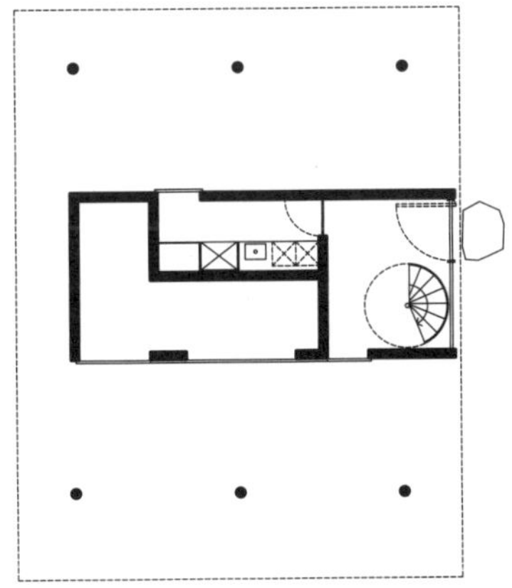

Lantern House
Waiheke
2018

When the project came to us, we inherited a building site—a big cut into the land, supported by a retaining wall. We decided not to use this cut as the platform for the house; instead, it became a sheltered courtyard behind the house, which could then be cantilevered forward towards the sea.

An orthodox response to sites such as this is to put a deck at the front of the house. What you then see when looking out from the house is an expanse of deck and a balustrade in the foreground of a distant view, not the view you really want. You want to be able to look out to the ocean and also down at the rocks beneath you without having to go to the edge of a deck to do so. The decision to go forward not with a deck but with the house itself allowed for a more dramatic engagement with the coastal environment. Though sheltered, the courtyard is also connected to the wider setting via the house's framed views of Onetangi Bay.

At the entrance to the site is a mature pōhutukawa, which we had to work around. The road is at this level and our first idea—quite a mid-century one—was to bring cars in here. You would drive into a 'lantern', similar to the batten structure at Clevedon Estate, and then step down into the building. At the clients' request, that arrival space was given over to accommodation, but the lantern name, and notion, survived.

There is quite a lot of fracturing of the house's forms, and sliding and hiding of glass within the skin. Vertical screens in front of the main bedroom are a means of differentiating private from public space, while retaining the prospect from the room. Most clients might have insisted on uninterrupted glazing, but this house's owners were supportive of a less obvious window treatment. LH•NH

Upper Floor
Lower Floor

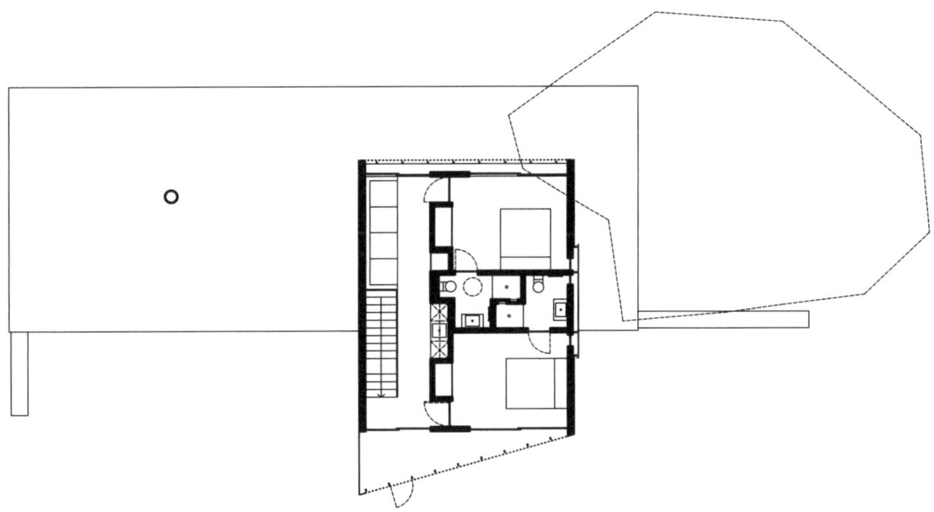

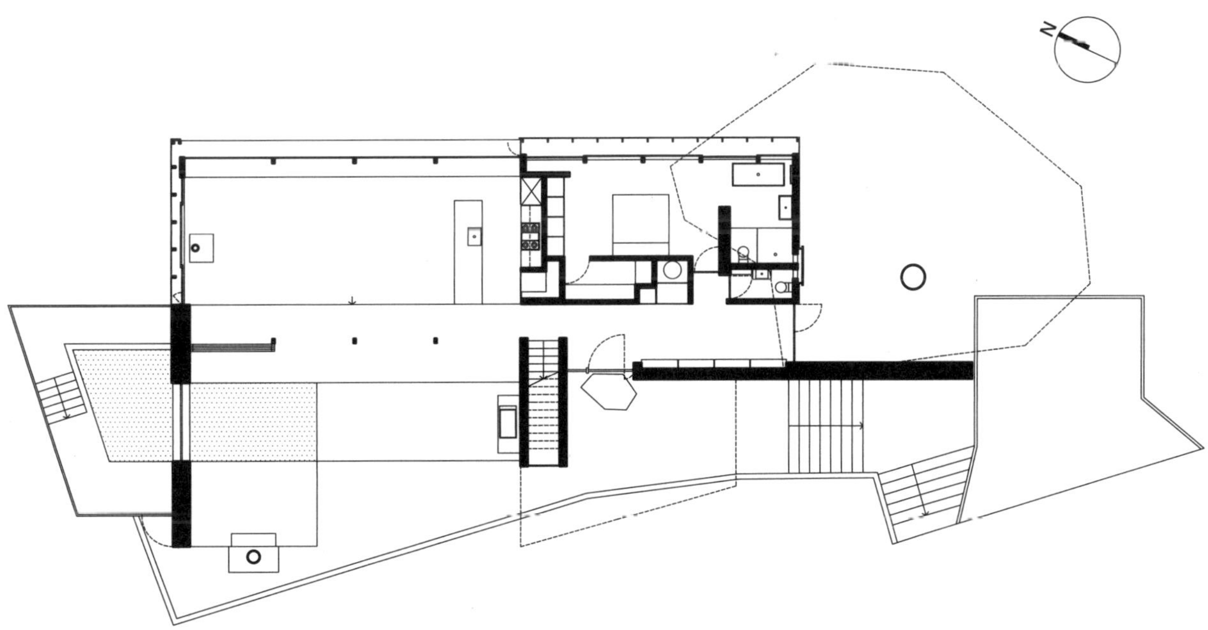

Dune House
Leigh
2021

The house sits in the rolling dunes of a white sand beach about an hour and a half north of Auckland. At the beach, a 100-metre building setback means that to get a sea view a house must achieve a certain elevation. A double-storey building sticking up above the long line of the dunes, though, would be transgressive, even if it were permissible. We decided to lower the house by raising the ground. The house was placed on piles, about three metres above ground level, and the land was then recontoured to meet the top of the piles. The result is a double-height house that presents as a single-level building.

The house is really a diagram of going as high as is possible, or desirable, in a sensitive landscape, taking a lead from the horizontality of that landscape and softening the form and impact of the building with a screen. The concept for the screen is the inversion or mirroring of the surrounding dunes. At the time we were working on this house there was a renewed interest in the arch as a design element. On Dune House, we wanted to experiment with the arch, in a playful or subversive way, as a means of referencing and connecting with the immediate landscape.

We've never believed beach houses should be glass houses, and have devoted a lot of effort to devising ways to hide glazing when the weather allows some or all of a house to be opened up. In Dune House the parking spaces for the glass are deep pockets into which two panels can slide. The batten screen of the house also reduces the glare of the glazing. The screen started out as a scribble; design doesn't often happen this way, but this time it did. The form of the screen is organic and soft—the arch as a lacy, drooped skirt. The geometry of the screen is quite complicated, and beautifully made and detailed. If you have a singular idea, you have to execute it really well. LH•NH

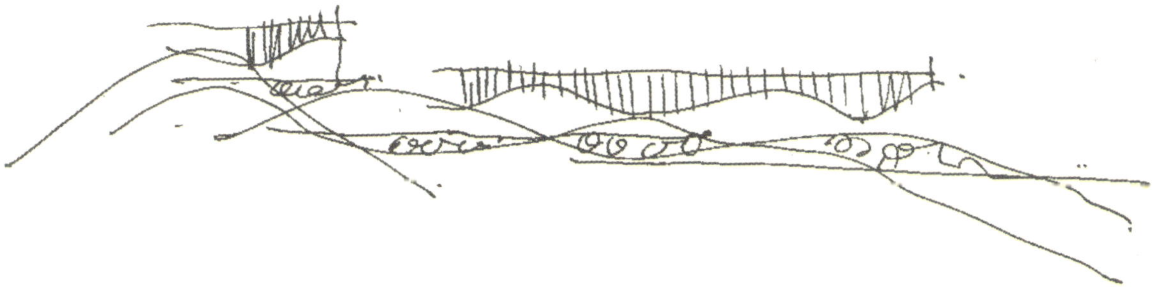

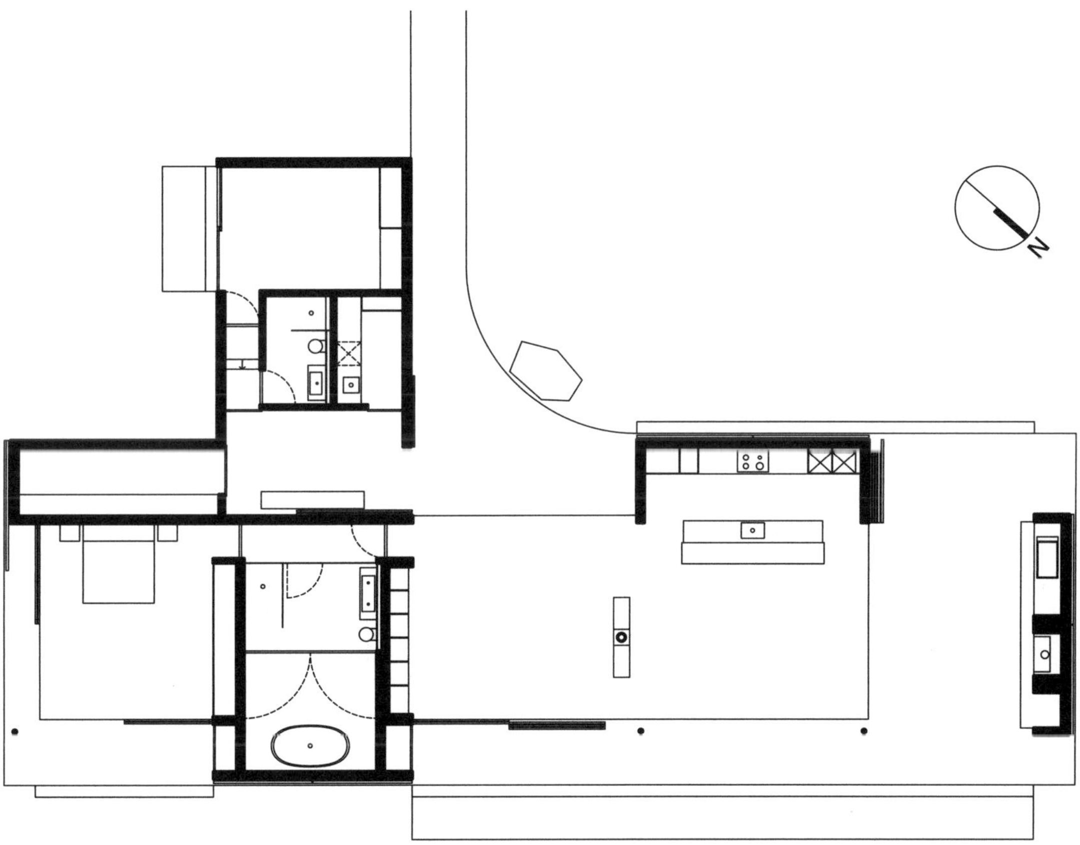
N

Awana Beach House
Aotea Great Barrier
2020

The house is prominently sited above the tideline on a publicly accessible beach and we were very aware of local sensitivities when we designed it, especially as for much of the time the house would be observed in an unoccupied state. Because of this context, designing the building became very much a matter of envisaging what it would look like when it wasn't being used. We gave the house an entire skin of moveable shutters that reduce its reflectivity, conceal its interior and lessen its mass. The timber screens were intended to weather and fade into the natural colours of the site.

Awana Beach, like Aotea in general, gets a lot of weather. As well as enabling the house to defer to its setting, the shutters serve as barrier layers against wind, sea spray and the roar of the surf. On this project, the shutters were upsized; their dimensions—they are three-and-a-half metres high—and the house's demanding maritime environment required frames and tracking systems made of aircraft-grade aluminium. The scale of the shutters is consistent with the design strategy of having the house address the beach as a single-storey structure; behind the tall screen of its beach elevation the house retreats up into the site's two-metre incline.

The lanai is the heart of the plan, a one-and-a-half storey volume in the middle of the building where the rear pavilion on its east–west axis intersects with the front pavilion on its north–south axis. This was the first time we locked a lanai inside a building, although the space may be opened on both its north and south sides to external courtyards. As well as providing a sheltered internal courtyard—a place of retreat on a relentless coast—the lanai is the means to manage the level change between the front and rear pavilions.

We had always been concerned to give beach houses, even small baches, some ballast that would embed them in their site and signal a sense of belonging. Hence our frequent use of gabion walling. At Awana Beach House, a bigger building directly confronting the elements, stone is used more substantially to support the plinth on which the building sits. LH•NH

Upper Floor
Lower Floor

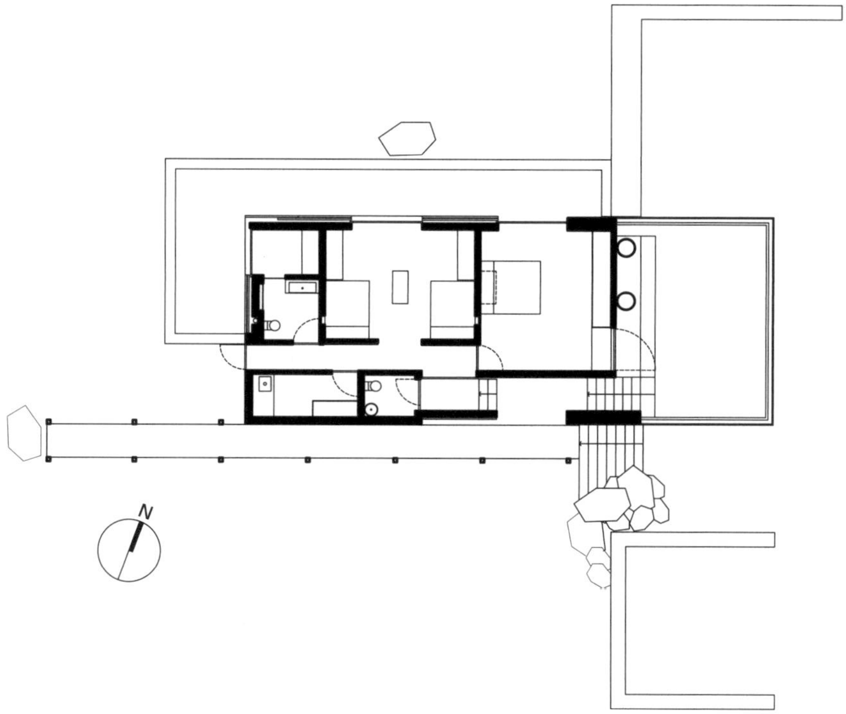

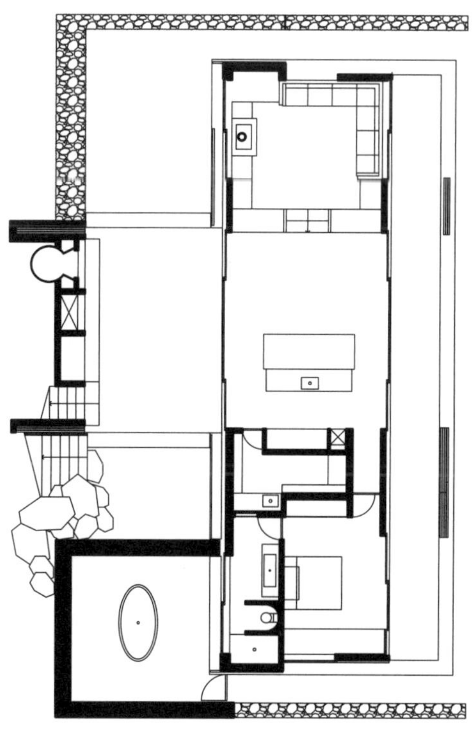

213

Omata Beach House
Northland
2022

The house, sited on the coast of a remote 315-hectare property in the far north of New Zealand, shows how far our beach architecture has come since our early 'sticky' baches. Some change has been inevitable; larger houses are necessarily more solid structures, and amendments to New Zealand's building code have required heftier detailing.

However, as we dealt with technical challenges, our design thinking was also evolving. On a visit to the Greek islands, we were impressed by buildings designed by modern architects. These architects were working in a masonry tradition, not just piling stone on stone, but using stone as contour, which of course is also part of the classical tradition of Greek architecture. The nouns in this architectural language are stone, rock, earth. We had always been concerned with anchoring our houses; now, we became much more interested in cutting and digging into the landscape, which is a way of building that also has its own history in Aotearoa.

The house sits against an escarpment, as close as possible to the beach while being sufficiently elevated above the high-water mark and surge level. A stone plinth supports the timber house—the Acropolis to its Parthenon. The building is not so much grounded as it is the generator of its own ground. In the dormitory wing, all bedrooms look out to the bay and have their own individual terraces. These bedrooms, like the house's other spaces, are simply appointed, with a disciplined palette of materials. The house is not small, but it's not baggy or excessive. There's a lanai—our familiar transitional space—protected by a sophisticated system of rain screens and shutters so that it may function day and night, in sunshine or rain.

We wanted to try something different with the roof and believed an inverted, or subverted, arch would give character to a pavilion. It would do other things, too. Omata Beach House is a light building on a heavy base, with a lot of glass behind its screens and shutters; in the absence of edges, the inverted arch serves to hold space. Flipped up towards the afternoon sun, it also acknowledges the bay. We wanted to achieve a balance of shelter and freedom. LH•NH

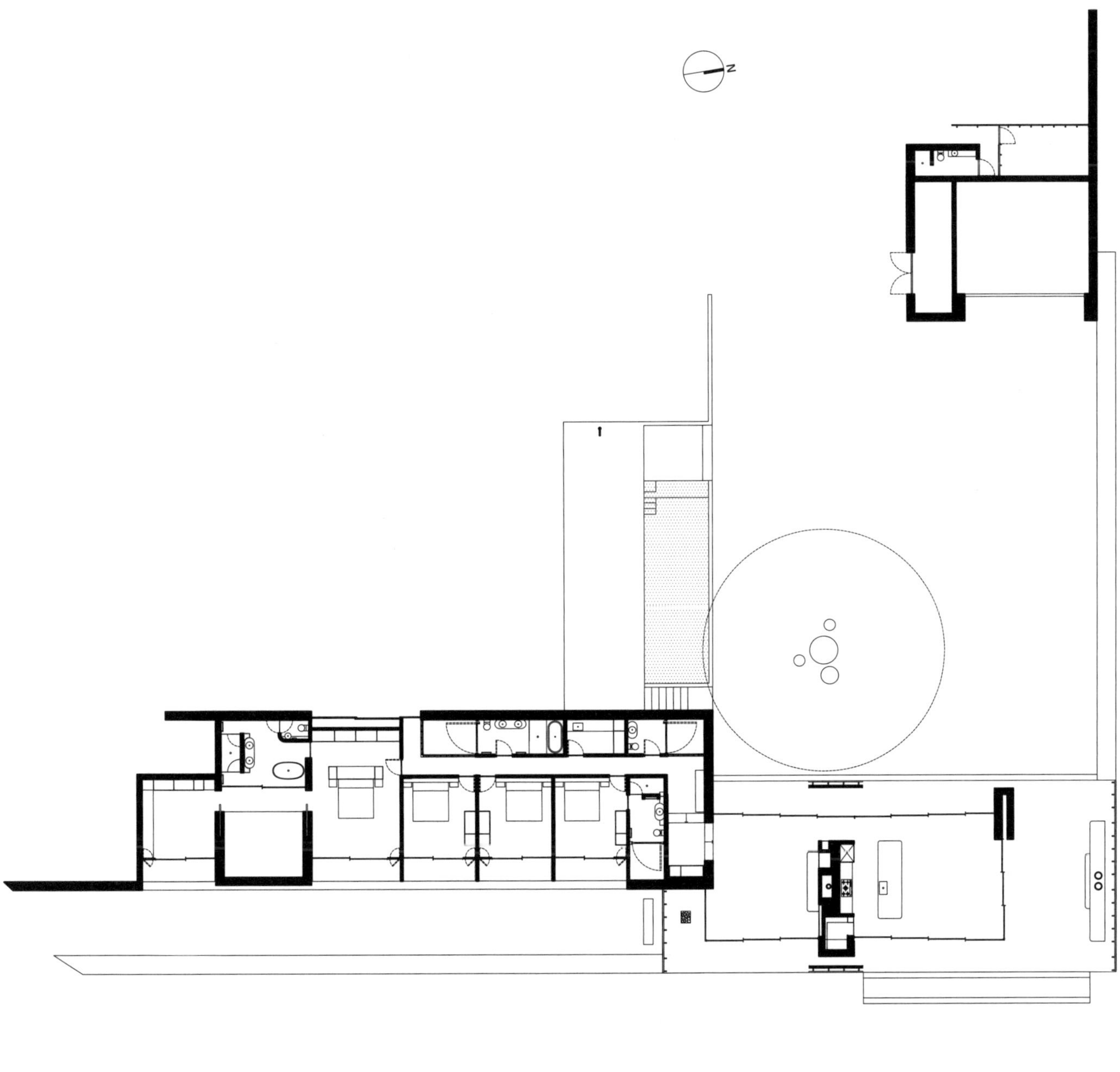

Architecture Awards (From Te Kāhui Whaihanga New Zealand Institute of Architects)

2023

- Omata Beach House:
  Sir Ian Athfield Award for Housing
  New Zealand Award
  Auckland Award
- Omata Hill House:
  Auckland Award

2022

- Matapōuri House:
  Auckland Award
- Rangiputa Bach:
  Auckland Award

2020

- Papamoa Beach House:
  Waikato/Bay of Plenty Award
- Tūtūkākā House:
  Auckland Award

2018

- Kawakawa House:
  Sir Ian Athfield Award for Housing
  New Zealand Award
  Auckland Award
- Lantern House:
  Auckland Award
- Mission Bay Pavilion Restaurant:
  Auckland Awards (Hospitality & Heritage)

2017

- Bethells Bach:
  Auckland Award

2016

- Bramasole:
  New Zealand Award
  Auckland Award
- Kauaeranga Valley House:
  New Zealand Award
  Waikato/Bay of Plenty Award

2015

- Castle Rock House:
  New Zealand Award
  Auckland Award
- Clevedon Estate:
  New Zealand Award
  Auckland Award

2011

- Kaitoke Bach:
  Auckland Award
- Under Pōhutukawa:
  New Zealand Award
  Auckland Award
- Wetland Folly Aotea:
  Auckland Award

2009

- Inside Out Bach Aotea:
  Auckland Award
- Via Centro:
  Auckland Award

2008

- Bark House:
  Waikato/Bay of Plenty Award
- Ōruawharo Bay Bach:
  New Zealand Award

2005

- Hammerhead House:
  Auckland Award

2002

- Herbst Bach Aotea:
  New Zealand Award
  Auckland Award
- Island Bach Aotea:
  Auckland Award
- Parnell School Library:
  Auckland Award

Te Kāhui Whaihanga New Zealand Institute of Architects (NZIA) is the society representing most of the architects and architecture graduates and students in Aotearoa New Zealand. Founded in 1905, it was gifted its Māori name in 2019. The NZIA's peer-reviewed awards programme has operated for nearly a century.

People

From its inception, Herbst Architects has benefitted from the contribution of talented architects and graduates. The following design practitioners have worked in the studio:

André Fourie
Sianne Smith
Ryan Mahon
Emily Stephens
Fraser McNaught
Alyssa Aisyah
Bodie Maxcey
Hannah Sharp
Anna Boow
Jimmy Gray
Declan Burn
Paul Davidson
Jeremy Priest
Daniel Smith
Yvette Overdyke
Mat Brown
Jeff Brickell
James Craig
Alex Schwab
Katie Newall
Gabriel Fung
Zhenyu Li
Kate Beilby
Pru Pinfold
Liselotte Knall
Madushin Amarasekera
Yi-Jan Lien
Rochelle Mahon

Acknowledgements

The author and Herbst Architects wish to acknowledge the current and former owners of the houses presented in this book; Alan Deare and Anna Wilkinson of Area Design, the book's designers; and The Warren Trust, a valued supporter of architectural publishing in Aotearoa.

About the author

John Walsh is a writer who specialises in architecture. He edited *Architecture New Zealand* magazine for a decade, has contributed to numerous periodicals and is the author of several books on New Zealand architecture. He edited the publications accompanying the New Zealand exhibition at the 2014 and 2016 Venice Architecture Biennale and latterly has written guides to the architecture of Auckland (2021), Wellington (2022) and Christchurch (2023).

Photographers

Simon Devitt

Clevedon Estate

Sam Hartnett

Kawakawa House

Jackie Meiring

Herbst Bach
Ōruawharo Bay Bach
Kaitoke Bach
Lantern House
Awana Beach House

Patrick Reynolds

Ōruawharo Bay Bach
Under Pōhutukawa
Castle Rock House
Kauaeranga Valley House
Kawakawa House

Simon Wilson

Dune House
Omata Beach House

MASSEY UNIVERSITY PRESS

The Warren Trust

First published in 2024 by
Massey University Press
Private Bag 102904
North Shore Mail Centre
Auckland 0745, New Zealand
www.masseypress.ac.nz

A catalogue record for this book is available from the National Library of New Zealand